DOUBLE VISION: HIDDEN MEANINGS

IN THE PROPHECY OF ISAIAH

Brian Johnston

Copyright © 2018 Hayes Press

Published by

HAYES PRESS Publisher, Resources & Media

The Barn, Flaxlands

Royal Wootton Bassett

Swindon, SN4 8DY

United Kingdom

www.hayespress.org

Table of Contents

CHAPTER 1 - THE SHAME AND THE GLORY

It's often the case that something we have doesn't appear shabby until we see it beside something else which is brand new. It's then we become painfully aware of the difference, and we can be very embarrassed or even ashamed. In the days of the Bible prophet Isaiah, the condition of God's people had become more than shabby. It was shameful – to the extent that in the first five chapters of Isaiah God denounces the condition of his people like this:

> "Woe to those who call evil good, and good evil; who put darkness for light, and light for darkness; who put bitter for sweet, and sweet for bitter! Woe to those who are wise in their own eyes, and prudent in their own sight! Woe to men mighty at drinking wine ... Who ... take away justice from the righteous man! They have rejected the law of the LORD of hosts, and despised the word of the Holy One of Israel" (Isaiah 5:20-24 NKJV).

Perhaps most people had grown used to it, but this was the deplorable state of affairs that'd existed during king Uzziah's reign (2 Chronicles 26) - during which time Isaiah had begun to witness and speak up for God. Near the end of his reign, even king Uzziah failed to set a good example. Losing sight of the holiness and glorious character of God, the king had boldly gone where no king ought ever to go. He entered into God's temple on earth to do what was only permitted to the priests to do. As a result, he was struck down with leprosy and died after being quarantined in this state that was regarded as 'unclean' in those days.

It may have been that when the king died the prophet Isaiah came up to the great temple of God in Jerusalem. It was a time of mourning, uncertainty and crisis. It was also the time that he got a vision, a revelation, of the glory of God in God's heavenly temple. It's this, and the impression it made on him, which he records for us in chapter 6:1-3:

> "In the year that King Uzziah died, I saw the Lord sitting on a throne, high and lifted up, and the train of His robe filled the temple. Above it stood seraphim; each one had six wings: with two he covered his face, with two he covered his feet, and with two he flew. And one cried to another and said: "Holy, holy, holy is the LORD of hosts; the whole earth is full of His glory!"

In stark contrast to the shame of the people, and the dark depths to which they'd sunk, this was a revelation that shone with the brightness of the glory of God. In fact because of the sad and shameful state of the people, the visible glory of God was set to depart from the temple at Jerusalem. Another prophet, Ezekiel, was later going to describe its departure. Because of that, we might ask here: 'In what sense was the whole earth full of God's glory?' Would any answer not have to include the glory of God's judgements? Remember the time when God's people, Israel, disobeyed and disbelieved that God could bring them into the promised land. It was then God said:

> "... as I live, all the earth shall be filled with the glory of the LORD – because all these men who have seen My glory and the signs which I did in Egypt and in the wilderness, and have put Me to the test now these ten times, and have not heeded My voice, they certainly shall not see the land of which I swore to their fathers, nor shall any of those who rejected Me see it" (Numbers 14:21-23 NKJV).

In Isaiah's day, the time was again fast approaching when God would judge his people, and in that judgement the glory of his holy name would be upheld. As Isaiah continued to watch the unfolding revelation, he said:

> "Woe is me, for I am undone! Because I am a man of unclean lips, and I dwell in the midst of a people of unclean lips; for my eyes have seen the King, the LORD of hosts." Then one of the seraphim flew to me, having in his hand a live coal which he had taken with the tongs from the altar. And he touched my mouth with it, and said: "Behold, this has touched your lips; your iniquity is taken away, and your sin purged" (Isaiah 6:5-7).

In the glorious light of God's holiness displayed in the temple, Isaiah saw his own shortcomings more clearly than ever before. Remember, this wasn't the beginning of his service and witness for God, but this was definitely a deepening of his experience in preparation for a special task of testifying to the people. Sometimes we, too, can let our standards be influenced by those of society around us. Then, all at once, when reading our Bibles prayerfully, our hearts are challenged by a greater revelation of the glorious holiness of God. At such moments when God draws near, what can we do but confess our unworthiness, our uncleanness, and realize afresh our total indebtedness to the cleansing work of the Lord upon the cross when he purged our sins by his death (Hebrews 1:3)? God cleanses us to use us. No doubt Isaiah's confession of his uncleanness reflected back upon the situation of the king who'd just died as an unclean leper. But when the call to serve came, Isaiah was ready:

> "Also I heard the voice of the Lord, saying: "Whom shall I send, and who will go for Us?" Then I said, "Here am I! Send me." And He said, "Go, and tell this people: 'Keep on hearing, but do not understand; keep on seeing, but do not perceive.' "Make the heart of this people dull, and their ears heavy, and shut their eyes; lest they see with their eyes, and hear with their ears, and understand with their heart, and return and be healed" (Isaiah 6:8-10).

So the message Isaiah was to preach wouldn't be popular – something that was still the case in the days of Christ's own preaching (Matthew 3:14,15). It, too, would not be well-received. Isaiah's success, if we can call it that, wouldn't be measured in terms of fruitfulness, but in terms of his faithfulness to his mission. I wonder if that's how we see it today – as we share the Christian message of repentance toward God and faith in the Lord Jesus Christ?

Any attempt to change the contents of the message to make it more popular and attractive to human thought, only serve to make it a different Gospel (Galatians 1:6). Any today who preach too low a view of God; too light a view of sin; and any for whom the cross isn't central, need to think long and hard about the revelation Isaiah got. Isaiah himself reacted by saying to God:

> "Lord, how long?" And He answered: "Until the cities are laid waste and without inhabitant, the houses are without a man, the land is utterly desolate ... But yet a tenth will be in it, and will return and be for consuming, as a terebinth tree or as an oak, whose stump remains when it is cut down. So the holy seed shall be its stump" (Isaiah 6:11-13 NKJV).

Isaiah, like Paul later (Romans 11:2), knew God hadn't cast off his people for ever. But this was God's judgement on people who'd become hardened against what he had to say to them. When Isaiah heard what a thankless task it would be, no wonder he asked how long he'd have to sustain this ministry. Yet there'd still be one in ten with responsive hearts! Even if it's a while since we knew the joy of reaping, let's be encouraged that God's preserved some with responsive hearts today too.

The ten percent of Jews who would return to God were to pass through a time of trouble. They'd return and be 'consumed', that is be 'eaten' or 'burnt up'. The books of Ezra and Nehemiah tell us that's how it turned out for those who returned to rebuild Jerusalem after God judged it at the hand of the Babylonians in the sixth century BC. After that captivity a remnant, a small proportion, of Israel returned to God. It'll be the same for Israel in a time that's still future when they're troubled by the Antichrist (Jeremiah 30:7).

After that future great tribulation for Israel a returning remnant will again be saved. This is what we mean by Isaiah's double vision. His predictions were not only near-sighted, but far-sighted too. Many times in this series we'll see how his prophecies have a double fulfillment: one in the past, the other still future for Israel. What's more, there are lessons in principle we can learn from then for this present time! Not long after king Uzziah's death, Rome was founded.

Yes, the power of Rome was coming, another power that was destined to wield authority over Jerusalem. That's already happened in history, of course. At the time of Christ's birth, Rome was the ruling power, but in the end-times still to come, a European power, in many ways equivalent to Rome, will be dominating events in Jerusalem. Then at the Second Advent of Christ, a future remnant of Israel will be delivered despite their present state of being hardened against the Gospel. How delightful to think of Isaiah's heart-breaking service of witnessing which yielded little or no apparent result, finally bearing fruit in a day still to come when Israel returns again to God. Her faith will have been severely tested, but finally she'll be prepared to embrace the one whose glory Isaiah saw (John 12:41). Be encouraged as you witness, Christian friend, only eternity will reveal the results of faithful years of testifying.

CHAPTER 2 - THE VIRGIN SHALL CONCEIVE

It's the prophet Isaiah who supplies us with two of the most famous verses that many associate with Christmas. Let's explore them in their original context first. In the book of Isaiah, chapter 7, we read: "It was told to the house of David, saying, "Syria's forces are deployed in Ephraim." ...Then the LORD said to Isaiah, "Go out now to meet Ahaz ... at the end of the aqueduct from the upper pool, on the highway to the Fuller's Field..."

Perhaps Ahaz, king of the southern part of Israel (or Judah), was assessing his defences, checking that his water supply was secure from the opposing forces of Syria and the northern part of Israel, also known as Ephraim. But, following God's instruction to him, the prophet Isaiah was to give the king a better reassurance than his own defences could provide that day: "Thus says the Lord GOD: "It shall not stand, [that's the enemy's plans shall not come to pass] ..."

God said that king Ahaz need not fear either the Syrians or the Israelites to the north. However, if Ahaz didn't believe the message, neither would he be established. To encourage his faith, God: "...spoke again to Ahaz, saying, "Ask a sign for yourself from the LORD your God; ask it either in the depth or in the height above." But Ahaz said, "I will not ask, nor will I test the LORD!" Then he said, "Hear now, O house of David! Is it a small thing for you to weary men, but will you weary my God also? Therefore the Lord Himself will give you a sign: Behold, the virgin shall conceive and bear a Son, and shall call His name Immanuel. Curds and honey He shall eat, that He may know to refuse the evil and choose the good. For before the Child shall know to refuse the evil and choose the good, the land that you dread will be forsaken by both her kings" (Isaiah 7:10-16 NKJV).

What was this sign? And how did it relate to the impending danger? Remember, an invasion was threatened. The march of the allied armies had commenced. Jerusalem was in consternation, and Ahaz had gone forth to see if there were any means of defence. Isaiah had been sent to him by God to assure him that there was no cause for fear at that moment. It was not to assure him that the nation should be ultimately and finally safe, but the pledge was, that he had no reason to fear "this" invasion. Christians have no doubt that this sign of Immanuel has its greatest meaning with reference to the birth of Jesus Christ. Matthew in the first chapter of his Gospel (1:22-23) makes it clear that these words of Isaiah had a "fulness" of meaning in connection with the actual circumstances of the birth of Jesus Christ the long-awaited Messiah.

Isaiah's prophecy was not completely fulfilled until applied to one born of Mary while she was still a virgin. The ultimate message of deliverance – far beyond the deliverance offered to king Ahaz - was sealed by this sign of Immanuel – the virgin conceiving. Jesus of Nazareth, who was born to Mary before her marriage to Joseph was consummated, is the only one who can save us from the wages that our sins deserve before a holy God.

But was Matthew intending us to understand that this was the primary, the original, the exclusive meaning of the prophecy? Christ's coming more than seven hundred years after the time of Isaiah and Ahaz was no insurance against the Babylonian invasion of the sixth century BC – how then could it have been any assurance to Ahaz against the even more imminent threat of invasion from Syria and Samaria? Are we not back again to another example of Isaiah's double vision?

In the next chapter, Isaiah describes himself and his children as being 'signs' to the people at that time (see Isaiah 8:18). The theme of chapter 7 continues into the early verses of the eighth chapter, and seems to give further assurance about the prediction of the land being delivered from the invasion that was then threatening. Isaiah writes:

> "Then I went to the prophetess, and she conceived and bore a son. Then the LORD said to me ... before the child shall have knowledge to cry 'My father' and 'My mother', the riches of Damascus and the spoil of Samaria will be taken away before the king of Assyria" (Isaiah 8:3-4 NKJV).

It's the same point that's being made, the same assurance of deliverance. Once again we read that before a child would have 'knowledge to say, My father, and my mother,' or in other words, be able to discern between good and evil (Isaiah 7:16), 'the riches of Damascus and the spoil of Samaria' would be 'taken away before the king of Assyria.' It seems natural to relate this to what's just been said in the previous chapter, doesn't it? - a fulfilment that should've been satisfactory to Ahaz. Was Isaiah married, possibly remarried, at this time to 'a young woman of marriageable age'? We're simply not told the details of the first fulfilment of this special sign. But making sense of the passage seems to require that some child born at the time of Ahaz would have 'Immanuel' – 'God with us' - as an additional name or title, like Jesus of Nazareth later did.

But let me be absolutely clear that nothing we're saying takes anything away from the totally unique conception of Jesus Christ. Although the original word used by Isaiah could mean 'a young woman of marriageable age', the Holy Spirit in the New Testament confirms that its application to Mary the mother of the Lord was to a virgin in the full sense. Before Mary and Joseph "came together she was found to be with child by the Holy Spirit" (Matthew 1:18).

In this way we're confronted with the wonderful miracle of God's working in sending His Son to earth. In the miracle of 'the Word becoming flesh' – which many celebrate at this time of year – we accept by faith that the child born and cradled that day in the manger at Bethlehem was a child bearing undiminished deity. Indeed, as Isaiah moves on into the ninth chapter of his message, he emphasizes for us the fact that the child born is the son given: the gift of the eternal Son of God. Once again these famous words are set within a great prophetic sweep of history.

> "... the land of Zebulun and the land of Naphtali ... by the way of the sea, beyond the Jordan, in Galilee of the Gentiles. The people who walked in darkness have seen a great light; those who dwelt in the land of the shadow of death, upon them a light has shined. You

have multiplied the nation and increased its joy ... For You have broken the yoke of his burden... as in the day of Midian.

For every warrior's sandal from the noisy battle, and garments rolled in blood, will be used for burning and fuel of fire. For unto us a Child is born, unto us a Son is given; and the government will be upon His shoulder. And His name will be called wonderful, Counselor, Mighty God, everlasting Father, Prince of Peace. Of the increase of His government and peace there will be no end, upon the throne of David and over His kingdom, to order it and establish it with judgment and justice from that time forward, even forever" (Isaiah 9:1-7 NKJV).

Isaiah begins by speaking about a light in the darkness. That's what the coming of Christ was. Paul could speak of "the grace of God appearing [or actually 'shining forth" and "bringing salvation' (Titus 2:11); while John opens his Gospel by talking about "the true Light ... coming into the world" (John 1:9). By faith, we can all come to recognize the 'Son given' in the 'child born'. God gave his Son to be our Saviour – the only one in whom – by faith – we can receive the forgiveness of our sins before God. How can he forgive sins? Because he went on to pay for them in his blood at the cross, where he died taking the punishment for sin. The sign of Immanuel was a sign that was both 'deep as Sheol' and 'high as heaven' (Isaiah 7:11) for Jesus

Christ went down into death, but Sheol couldn't hold him in death, and he rose the third day and ascended to his Father's throne on high in heaven.

But again, Isaiah sees the coming of Christ in Jewish terms. Remember he lived in days of insecurity, lived with the threat of invasion. Nothing is more common in Isaiah than for him to begin a prophecy with reference to some remarkable deliverance which was soon to occur, and to end it by a statement of events connected with a higher deliverance under the Messiah.

When Isaiah wrote in these surrounding verses of the nation of Israel being multiplied, the prediction is still awaiting its final fulfillment when Christ returns to reign on this earth. Mention of the 'warrior's sandal', 'the noisy battle', 'the garments rolled in blood' match with the Bible's other descriptions of the great future campaign of Armageddon (Joel 3; Zechariah 14; Revelation 16). All of Israel's future victory, deliverance and joy is based on the birth of Christ. From Isaiah's double vision, we come back today to a single focus on the virgin-conceived child who is God's eternal Son given for us. Our victory, deliverance and joy is also based on the birth of that one child.

CHAPTER 3 - A FRESH START

———

The section of Isaiah we come to in this chapter is all about a fresh start, and it directs us to the person of Jesus Christ. In the time of the prophet Isaiah, the house and family of David among the people of Israel had degenerated so badly that they resembled the stump of a tree after it's been cut down. Isaiah describes them as the stem or stock of a tree: "Then a shoot will spring from the stem of Jesse, and a branch from his roots will bear fruit" (Isaiah 11:1). So the news wasn't all bad by any means. Because out of the stem or stump new growth would come: for a fresh green twig would grow to take the place of the whole trunk. And you'll remember there was a second picture: a branch (or shoot) would develop from the earth-covered roots of this stump. That reminds me of something I heard about while in Ireland recently.

A friend there was telling me of how he and his father had been digging peat once. They came across the branch of a tree lying buried about seven feet down in the peat. There was no sign of life about it, and they'd no idea how long it'd been buried – but it would have been some considerable time. They left it exposed to the air, and when they came back to it twelve months later they were amazed to find that a twelve-inch green shoot had developed from this dead-looking part of the long-buried old tree.

It's like that here in Isaiah, with this picture of a fresh start after a long period of degeneration. What's more, Isaiah's picture is exciting because it was about the coming of Christ – Christ coming to revive the fortunes of Israel. Yes, Isaiah's prophecy would lie buried underneath seven hundred years of history before coming to fruition with the arrival of Christ. It seems indicated that the word used here for this shining new growth ('netzar' – a shoot, from 'natzar' – to shine) connects with the prediction that Jesus would be a 'Nazarene' (Matthew 2:23). There then follows a glorious description of the excellencies that were found in Jesus of Nazareth. For Isaiah goes on to say: "And the Spirit of the LORD will rest on Him, the spirit of wisdom and understanding, the spirit of counsel and strength, the spirit of knowledge and the fear of the LORD" (v.2).

It's the Spirit of God in his sevenfold fullness resting upon Christ! In fact, this is the first of three great statements Isaiah makes about the Holy Spirit in connection with Jesus Christ. The reference here in chapter 11, the one we've read, is related to the Lord's birth; whereas the mention in chapter 42 of God's Spirit being put upon Jesus as God's servant takes us to the time of the Lord's baptism (Luke 3:22); and the third and last mention, in chapter 61, brings us to the beginning of the Lord's public ministry and how the Lord spoke out in the synagogue at Nazareth about the fact he was anointed to preach the good news (Luke 4:18).

Throughout the life of Jesus Christ, Isaiah's words were true of him: "He will delight in the fear of the LORD" (v.3). Old Testament experts (like W.E. Vine) tell us it's quite proper to read that as 'the fear of the LORD shall be fragrance to him'. I like that: the fear of the LORD was fragrance to Jesus. In this same way, sin was odious to him. The New Testament tells us that he "loved righteousness and hated lawlessness" (Hebrews 1:9). His disciple Peter preached about him that: "He went about doing good ... healing all who were oppressed by the devil; for God was with Him" (Acts 10:38 NASB).

Now here's where Isaiah's double vision comes in. Prophecy is no respecter of time. Two parts of a prophecy can sit together on the same page, but two thousand years will lie between their fulfilments. And not only will all Bible prophecy be fulfilled, but some of it will be fulfilled more than once, and hundreds of years apart - this being the idea of Isaiah's "double vision". No sooner has Isaiah spoken of the first coming of Christ, which was to happen seven hundred years after he wrote about it – no sooner has he spoken of that, but he's gone on to tell us things Christ will do that haven't happened yet, but will take place at his second coming. Listen:

> "... with righteousness He will judge the poor, and decide with fairness for the afflicted of the earth ... And the wolf will dwell with the lamb, and the leopard will lie down with the kid, and the calf and the young lion and the fatling together; and a little boy will lead them. Also the cow and the bear will graze; their young will lie down together; and the lion will eat straw like the ox. And the nursing child will play by the hole of the cobra, and the weaned child will put his hand on the viper's den. They will not hurt

or destroy in all My holy mountain, for the earth will
be full of the knowledge of the LORD as the waters
cover the sea" (v.4-9).

When the Lord Jesus lived here on earth for some thirty-three
years or thereabouts, his life was the most wonderful life, full of
helpful miracles. The blind were made to see, and the lame to
walk, and so on, as we read in the four Gospels. When the Lord
stilled the storm, walked on water, and calmly rode donkeys
that'd never been broken in for riding, he showed his power over
the world of nature, but the kind of general transformation of
behaviour throughout the animal kingdom that Isaiah speaks
about never happened at that time.

That doesn't mean the prophecy failed. It's time hasn't come yet.
For this earth hasn't seen the last of Jesus Christ. He's coming
back to this earth, and every word of Isaiah's predictions will
be fulfilled, alongside the others that have already been fulfilled.
The actual fulfillment of these conditions in the animal kingdom
will be the natural outcome of the power and authority of Christ
on this earth. Yes, Isaiah was looking to the future when he
wrote: "Then it will come about in that day that the nations
will resort to the root of Jesse, who will stand as a signal for the
peoples; and His resting place will be glorious" (v.10).

Everyone will one day discover the true identity of Jesus Christ
as the Son of God. Isaiah began with him as the lowly branch
coming from the obscurity of the root of king David's line. As the
branch, he's pictured for us as David's offspring; but notice he's
from the root of David (even of Jesse) – he comes before David
- for he pre-dates David in that he's the eternal Son of God. In

Isaiah's root and branch picture, both the deity and humanity of Christ are seen. Isaiah sees this divine ruler as a king of peace for the earth. He will stand as a signal –as a banner – for the peoples of the world. Not like a banner that summons people to war, but drawing them to himself as the benign ruler, the bringer of peace to this war-torn planet.

Then it will happen on that day that the Lord will again recover the second time with His hand the remnant of His people, who will remain (v.11). We can't miss Isaiah's double vision when we reflect on Isaiah's expression: 'a second time'. Isaiah's prophecy for Israel would first be fulfilled at the time of the Bible book of Ezra. It's there we read of how a remnant would be recovered in the sixth century B.C. out of the captivity that lay ahead in Babylon. That was the first time the Lord would recover the remnant of his people. In the future context of Isaiah's words it'll happen a second time. Problems lie ahead for Israel and Jerusalem. They won't even be ended when a (three and a half year) peace deal is struck. Their problems will only end when the Lord they once rejected will take action "with his hand."

There can be no promise that this coming new year will be a year of peace for us personally. But the way to have lasting peace is to acknowledge by faith Jesus Christ as the Prince of Peace. Come to him, for as the chorus says, "his banner over us is love". He wants to recover your life from sin. Will you, then, resort to him? His hand is outstretched to you in peace – will you grasp it?

CHAPTER 4 - TO BABYLON AND BEYOND

―――

The message of the prophet Isaiah we'll be looking at in this chapter was directed against Lucifer or Satan, but it can be a bit confusing because Isaiah first of all seems to be talking about the king of Babylon. It's another aspect of what we're calling Isaiah's double vision. God has been explaining a few facts about the world superpower that was going to sweep Israel away in the sixth century B.C. Beginning in chapter one of Isaiah, God's already made clear that his people Israel are strong-willed and rebellious against him, and it's for this reason that he's going to allow the Babylonian Empire to teach Israel a lesson.

But he also made it clear he wouldn't tolerate the excessive cruelty people like the Babylonians were going to inflict on Israel. After using them as his instruments of judgement, God would break their power too. Then he would remember his mercy towards Israel in accordance with the promises he'd made to them long before. Finally, he'd bring things full circle, by using Israel as a channel of blessing for Gentile nations like the ones who'd been used to discipline her.

Many chapters in Isaiah show us how God uses the nations of the earth to serve his purpose, but at the same time, holds them responsible for how they go about it. In Isaiah's day, Israel's bitter medicine lay ahead. And God was going to use the Babylonians to dispense it. But he'd hold them accountable for the lengths to which they went. The king of Babylon was a proud, arrogant king who would also, in his turn, be judged by God. God uses him as a vehicle for revealing to us his judgement against the pride of Satan himself. So Isaiah was told to:

> "Take up this proverb against the king of Babylon, and say: "How the oppressor has ceased, the golden city ceased! ... he who ruled the nations in anger, is persecuted ...
>
> "Hell [i.e. Hades or Sheol] from beneath is excited about you, to meet you at your coming; it stirs up the dead for you ... They all shall speak and say to you: 'Have you also become as weak as we? Have you become like us? Your pomp is brought down to Sheol ... "How you are fallen from heaven, O Lucifer, son of the morning! How you are cut down to the ground, you who weakened the nations! For you have said in your heart: 'I will ascend into heaven, I will exalt my throne above the stars of God ... I will ascend above the heights of the clouds, I will be like the Most High.' Yet you shall be brought down to Sheol, to the lowest depths of the Pit'" (Isaiah 14:4-17 NKJV).

What a graphic account Isaiah gives us of the demise of this mighty man – in which the spirits of already departed ones are able to consciously recollect the kind of authority the king of Babylon wielded while he was alive. But now he's come to join them among the dead. Death is seen as the great equalizer. 'Have you become weak like us?' the spirits in Hades say to the newcomer. A solemn reminder to us all that a day of reckoning is coming, whereby: "It is appointed to men to die and after death comes judgement" (Hebrews 9:27).

And yet, beyond the doom of the Babylonian king, the doom of Lucifer himself is glimpsed. Lucifer or Satan begins to be addressed under the figure of the proud king of Babylon whom God was going to judge. So God also reveals his judgement against the Devil or Satan too. Satan's pride had been to boast: "I will ascend into heaven, I will exalt my throne above the stars of God". These examples serve to show that God knows how to bring the proud down low. The king of Babylon's power-base would also be destroyed, and he would have no lasting dynasty: "For I will rise up against them," says the LORD of hosts, "And cut off from Babylon the name and remnant, and offspring and posterity," says the LORD. "I will also make it a possession for the porcupine, and marshes of muddy water" (Isaiah 14:22-23 NKJV).

More double vision! After a captivity lasting seventy years, Jews would return to rebuild the Jerusalem destroyed by Babylon. They'd be able to do so because God would raise up the Medo-Persians to topple the power of Babylon. The city of Babylon did fall to the Medo-Persians. The Bible prophet Daniel lived to see Isaiah's prophecies come true. But we say "more double vision" because once again the city of Babylon exists in the modern world amid all the reconstruction work that's current in modern Iraq. Isaiah's prediction of the final and utter nature of Babylon's fall (especially in the chapter before this: Isaiah 13:19-22) belongs to the future. In this deeper sense, Isaiah was glimpsing what the apostle John saw and recorded in the final book of Revelation (chapters 16-19) – and that's still to happen. Isaiah's prophecies cover other nations too. In chapter 16 we find this appeal:

> "Let My outcasts dwell with you, O Moab; be a shelter to them from the face of the spoiler. For the extortioner is at an end, devastation ceases, the oppressors are consumed out of the land. In mercy the throne will be established; and One will sit on it in truth, in the tabernacle of David, judging and seeking justice and hastening righteousness" (Isaiah 16:4-5 NKJV).

This appeal to Moab is very interesting. It, too, has an application to the end-time still to come. When the coming strong-man of Europe begins to flex his muscles against Jerusalem, then there'll be the time the Lord Jesus spoke of in Matthew's Gospel chapter 24 (vv.20,21), when Jews will flee from their city and their land, fleeing from a greater tribulation than even they've known to date. Daniel, in the Old Testament, takes up the story: "He [Europe's tyrant] will ... enter the beautiful land [Israel], and many countries will fall; but these will be rescued out of his hand: Edom, Moab and the foremost of the sons of Ammon" (Daniel 11:41).

Satan will energise Europe's leader in his drive to exterminate the Jewish people, especially the small portion of them who are loyal to God. As they flee to the mountains of Moab from Jerusalem, the apostle John in his vision (Revelation 12) saw a flood – maybe representing a military expedition – sent out after them, but the earth swallows it up. The sandy nature of the area in question could easily be made to accomplish that. The deep rocky gorges surrounding places like Petra will give a safe refuge (for three and a half years) to the remnant of Jews who'll then form the nucleus of the race when Christ comes to set up his kingdom on earth. So this appeal to Moab through Isaiah to give Israel shelter will find a positive answer in a future day. Yet another nation Isaiah had a message for – this time in chapter 19 - was Egypt:

> "The burden against Egypt ... In that day five cities in the land of Egypt will speak the language of Canaan and swear by the LORD of hosts ... In that day there will be an altar to the LORD in the midst of the land of Egypt, and a pillar to the LORD at its border" (v.1,18,19).

Following Isaiah's usual pattern, we've the full range here from things which were about to happen through to events still future at the time when the Lord Jesus returns to this earth. Historically, there came a time when the language spoken in Canaan became the language spoken in Egypt, at least to the limited extent indicated. The Greek language that had become common in Canaan was adopted also in Egypt where the Greek translation of the Old Testament was produced. Even Judaism spread to Egypt where synagogues were built, for example at Heliopolis; and later still Christianity took a hold in Alexandria. But pointing further ahead to the time of Christ's Second Advent, we read of how: "... there will be a highway from Egypt to Assyria ... In that day Israel will be one of three with Egypt and Assyria - a blessing in the midst of the land" (Isaiah 19:23-24 NKJV).

So to one last example here of Isaiah's vision, this time from chapter 22:

> "Thus says the Lord GOD of hosts: "Go, proceed to this steward, to Shebna, who is over the house, and say: ... I will drive you out of your office ... I will call My servant Eliakim the son of Hilkiah; ... I will commit your responsibility into his hand ... The key of the house of David I will lay on his shoulder; so he shall open, and no one shall shut; and he shall shut, and no one shall open. I will fasten him as a peg in a secure place ... 'They will hang on him all the glory of his father's house ... all vessels of small quantity, from the cups to all the pitchers" (Isaiah 22:15-24 NKJV).

Soon after the time of the prophecy, this man Shebna, a sort of king's treasurer, was deposed from office in favour of Eliakim who was given even greater influence. But what's said of him, in a way, foreshadows what's true of Jesus Christ. Some of the things mentioned here are taken up by Christ himself in Revelation chapter 3 (verse 7) – about being able to open so that none can shut. Just as Eliakim replaced Shebna, Christ will replace the coming Antichrist. Jesus Christ is like that nail or peg fastened in a sure place on which at any time you can hang all your troubles, whether they're small ones like cups or much bigger troubles like pitchers. Shall we take this as an invitation to hang our troubles on the Lord Jesus to bear them for us?

CHAPTER 5 - PASSING THE TEST

G od's prophetic judgements against different nations like Moab and Egypt, spoken through Isaiah (in chapters 13-23), build up a real sense of a world ripening for divine judgement (cp. Revelation 14:15-19). But when do they refer to? Some of these judgements have already been fulfilled in history – that much is clear; but others are still future. Now, as Isaiah begins chapter 24, we're informed that those judgements that are still to happen will affect every level of society (v.2).

The earth is said to be defiled because they have "transgressed the laws, changed the ordinance, broken the everlasting covenant" (v.5). It seems likely that this connects in a special way with the time of the end, when Israel will align herself with the Antichrist: priding herself in a covenant with death and an agreement with hell (Isaiah 28:18). Isaiah predicts that "few men are left" (v.6). Global catastrophes will depopulate the earth to the extent that "unless the Lord had shortened those days, no flesh would be saved; but for the elect's sake, whom He chose, He shortened the days" (Mark 13:20). Grim days lie ahead for planet earth, with the disappearance of any trace of joy and mirth (vv.7-12). After the harvest of judgement, only a gleaning remains. That gleaning, that small leftover amount, represents a godly residue of Israel which again will have learnt to "sing for the majesty of the LORD" (v.14).

Then comes the open confession of a double treachery: Israel's betrayal of God through following the Antichrist will be the first; but the second treachery will be the Antichrist's betrayal of Israel by breaking his covenant, or peace deal, with them (v.16b; Daniel 9:27) – another twist in the road on Israel's tortuous journey to peace! One thing after another will come upon the world's inhabitants in these treacherous times. When we fail to understand Isaiah's prophecies in their double applications – future as well as past - we may be tempted to see the answer to them in the here and now: in the Church the Body of Christ. But, it's Israel, not the Church, that passes through this time of great trouble (Jeremiah 30:7). The note of victory struck at the end of chapter 24 with the LORD reigning on this earth is the same note struck again in chapter 27 – but the picture has changed; listen: "In that day the LORD will punish Leviathan the fleeing serpent, with His fierce and great and mighty sword, even Leviathan the twisted serpent; and He will kill the dragon who {lives} in the sea" (Isaiah 27:1 NASB).

That's exactly the kind of picture language the apostle John uses in the book of Revelation to tells us God will deal a decisive blow to the great dragon (compare Revelation 12:9; 20:2) - and we're left in no doubt there that he's speaking of the Devil - and that the time is still future. Christian hope is often expressed at funerals in the words of the apostle Paul to the Corinthians: "Death is swallowed up in victory" (Isaiah 25:8; 1 Corinthians 15:54). But these words are taken from Isaiah's prophecy in chapter 25. The truth of these words will be more obvious when Jesus reigns as king and human life span is again greatly extended.

And there's another preview of the eternal state, which we get when we read about God wiping away people's tears (Isaiah 25:8).

In a day to come, when God does that for Israel, they'll respond in worship saying: "This is our God" (Isaiah 25:9). In the light of all this, chapter twenty-six of Isaiah really belongs to the future. That's really what we're leading up to: chapter twenty-six of Isaiah belongs to the future. It's all about Israel expressing her sentiments after God has delivered them from the terrible trial of the Antichrist. But the thoughts it expresses often help and encourage us as Christians in any present difficulties. Let me remind you of perhaps the most famous verses of Israel's future song: "You will keep in perfect peace him whose mind is steadfast, because he trusts in you. Trust in the LORD for ever, for the LORD, the LORD, is the Rock eternal" (Isaiah 26:3-4 NIV).

How we've appreciated those words in our experience! Peace from God when stormy trials have been breaking around us - finding our security in the Rock of Ages in times of uncertainty. Israel herself will again sing this song of deliverance (see Revelation 15). As by the Red Sea shore when they were brought out of Egypt from Pharaoh (Exodus 15), so on the far side of their future sea of troubles a song of deliverance – of Moses and of the Lamb - will be raised. God gives songs in the night, the Bible says (Job 35:10). In the dark night of tribulation, the desire of Israel's soul will be kindled into song (26:9) – a song of praise to God.

Some of our greatest hymns have been born out of severely testing experiences for the hymn writer. We could mention Spafford, Matheson and Crosby, but there are many others who have taught us to sing praise through experiencing God as a very present help in any time of trouble (Psalm 46:1). They teach us to move from a sigh to a song. And, as part of her song, Israel will sing: "we have a strong city" (Isaiah 26:1). God weakened their strength in the way so that, in weakness, they might be made strong through depending on him (see Psalm 102:23). It's God who will keep the godly remnant of Israel in perfect peace in the intensity of trial. A mind that trusts steadfastly in God discovers the everlasting strength that's to be found in God. "In the way of Your judgements, O LORD, we have waited for You" (Isaiah 26:8), Israel sings, learning again that God rewards the patience of those who understand something of his purposes, and learn to await his time. Meekness is the inwrought grace of soul that enables us to accept God's dealings with us without complaining. And it's through meekness, that we come to the point of knowing God's purposes lie in the pathway of trial and testing.

Not that there's always, or even often, an understanding of how it's all "working for our [long-term] good" (Romans 8:28). But we don't need to be burdened with the detailed knowledge of "why?" since, as one tested believer expressed it: "the pattern of our life is His pattern, not ours". "I will seek You earnestly" (Isaiah 26:9) is still more of the lyrics of Israel's song. In a sense, trials free us from distractions. They're designed to have a sobering effect that rearrange our priorities and brings God closer. God's purpose is that of bringing us, like Job (chapter

42:5), to a greater sense of himself. In this way, some have come to describe their trial as a "glorious intruder". It was in the testing surroundings of a desert setting, that David developed a more acute thirst for God, expressed in seeking after Him (Psalm 63:1).

In a coming day, Israel's desire will not simply be for deliverance, but for the honour of God's great name (v.8). They can say: "Masters besides You have had dominion over us" (cp. 2 Chronicles 12:8). Yet only the LORD is memorable. He knows how to deliver the godly out of testing. When we – like Israel – learn that same truth, we glimpse the reality that trials are not only for refining our character, they can be for the glory of God too (John 9:3). Influencing others so that they glorify God (1 Peter 4:16) is part of the purpose.

With Israel, there's even talk of expansion – of the nation being increased (Isaiah 26:15). Like a tree, you and I as believers, grow strong in the dry times. In dry years a tree may show little sign of outward growth. Its trunk may gain no girth, and its crop of fruit may be shriveled. Deep beneath the soil, however, the roots are growing down in search of nourishing supplies of water. In these times the tree grows downwards, its roots penetrating deeper and deeper. Later, after some storm, people may wonder why this tree remains standing when many others around have fallen. So the lessons Israel still has to learn, when she passes through the trial of the great Tribulation, are all lessons which we, as believers, can learn now from the trials we may be called to pass through.

CHAPTER 6 – BEING TAUGHT A LESSON

―――

If we speak to adults in the way we speak to young children it can sound very patronising. Teaching adults as though they were children is precisely the situation we find in Isaiah chapter 28, but it's anything but patronising. During those dark days of Israel's history, their priests and prophets had become rather a smug lot – much like the self-satisfied and self-righteous scribes and Pharisees of a later date. They imagined themselves to be enlightened, but in reality, they were like children needing to be taught the basics one line at a time. Listen then to the irony of Isaiah's words directed against them:

> "Whom will he teach knowledge? And whom will he make to understand the message? Those just weaned from milk? Those just drawn from the breasts? For precept must be upon precept, precept upon precept, line upon line, line upon line, here a little, there a little. For with stammering lips and another tongue he will speak to this people, to whom He said, "This is the rest with which you may cause the weary to rest," and, "This is the refreshing"; yet they would not hear. But the word of the LORD was to them, "Precept upon precept, precept upon precept, line upon line, line upon line, here a little, there a little," that they might go and fall backward, and be broken and snared and caught" (Isaiah 28:9-29).

It was hardly adult education, was it? The religious experts who considered themselves so advanced, were really back in the nursery classroom. In fact, God was going to use foreigners to instruct them – "with stammering lips and another tongue he will speak to this people." God was going to speak to them in judgement at the hands of the Assyrians. And that, of course, is what did happen. While king Hezekiah was king in the south of the land, the Assyrians over-ran the north and brought the people to captivity.

But once again, Isaiah's words would have a second application much later in history. The apostle Paul quotes from this very section of Isaiah when writing his first letter to the Church of God at Corinth. In a sense the background is similar, for those who should have been at the stage of teaching God's Word were themselves behaving in a childish way:

> "And I, brethren, could not speak to you as to spiritual men, but as to men of flesh, as to babes in Christ. I gave you milk to drink, not solid food; for you were not yet able to receive it. Indeed, even now you are not yet able, for you are still fleshly. For since there is jealousy and strife among you, are you not fleshly, and are you not walking like mere men?" (1 Corinthians 3:1-3).

> "... Brethren, do not be children in your thinking; yet in evil be babes, but in your thinking be mature. In the Law it is written, "By men of strange tongues and

by the lips of strangers I will speak to this people, and even so they will not listen to Me," says the Lord" (1 Corinthians 14:20-21 NASB).

So this would appear to be a typical example of the dual fulfilment of prophecy. Firstly, the Assyrians with their foreign tongue would "speak against" Israel in judgement, taking them away into captivity. Then, hundreds of years later at Corinth, where there was a local Jewish community and trade centre, the early New Testament phenomenon of speaking in tongues also came to be seen as a fulfilment of this Isaiah prophecy. This might show that God's primary purpose in the use of the gift of tongues was directed towards unbelieving Jews – for there's no doubt that's the setting of Isaiah's original message. It seems that those of the "old order" – Jews who were very much attached to the law of Moses - were given this sign to prove that the new Christian revelation was of God.

A survey of the book of Acts tends to support this (think of the proselytes in Acts 2, Peter in Acts 10 and John's disciples in Acts 19) as being how the New Testament gift of tongues was also used - which points to a specific divine purpose at that particular time, does it not? Of the three recorded instances of tongues-speaking in the book of Acts (yes, there are only three!) we find in chapter 2 that it's the sign that marks the descent of the Holy Spirit at the dawn of that new era.

In chapter 10, it's the sign that emphasizes the fact that God was going to work equally with Gentiles in that new era. And finally, in chapter 19, it's the sign that underlines the further revelation to John's disciples concerning the new era. In other words, the

New Testament gift of tongues served a clear purpose at that specific time in history, when God was again speaking to his ancient, and generally unbelieving, people: the Jews. Returning to the Israelite leaders of Isaiah's day, never for one moment did they think God would use the Assyrians to express his judgements against them. They thought they had got their foreign policy sorted.

They thought they knew how to handle Egypt on the one hand and Assyria on the other. Israel, of course, lay between the regions of these great powers. Armies passing from either side would have to cross the land of Israel – and that's what they refer to as "the overflowing scourge" – but they boasted that they'd made deals with them and even outsmarted them. Just listen to their confidence:

> "... we have made a covenant with death, and with Sheol we are in agreement. When the overflowing scourge passes through, it will not come to us, for we have made lies our refuge, and under falsehood we have hidden ourselves." Therefore thus says the Lord GOD: "Behold, I lay in Zion a stone for a foundation, a tried stone, a precious cornerstone, a sure foundation; whoever believes will not act hastily [or will not be disturbed]. Also I will make justice the measuring line, and righteousness the plummet; the hail will sweep away the refuge of lies, and the waters will overflow the hiding place. Your covenant with death will be annulled, and your agreement with

Sheol will not stand; when the overflowing scourge
passes through, then you will be trampled down by it"
(vv.15-18).

Imagine going that far - to say they had no fear of death and
Hades! There's another indication here, one that ultimately
points forward to Israel's future agreement with the Antichrist.
The confidence of these self-deluded leaders was misplaced. They
boasted they were secure in their injustice and iniquity. But true
security belongs only to those who build their lives on Christ.
This is true now, as well as in the time of the end. Judgement
and righteousness will be God's plumb line to test everything.
God then directs his message, no longer to the defiant rebels, but
to those who were faithful among his people. He assures them,
through Isaiah, that God does not go on disciplining his faithful
ones indefinitely. The farmer knows when to stop ploughing and
God knows when to stop disciplining. Isaiah makes this same
point by asking questions:

> "Does the plowman keep plowing all day to sow?
> Does he keep turning his soil and breaking the clods?
> When he has leveled its surface, does he not sow the
> black cummin and scatter the cummin, plant the
> wheat in rows, the barley in the appointed place, and
> the spelt in its place? For He instructs him in right
> judgment, his God teaches him. For the black
> cummin is not threshed with a threshing sledge, nor
> is a cartwheel rolled over the cummin; but the black
> cummin is beaten out with a stick, and the cummin
> with a rod. Bread flour must be ground; therefore he

does not thresh it forever, break it with his cartwheel, or crush it with his horsemen. This also comes from the LORD of hosts, who is wonderful in counsel and excellent in guidance" (v.24-29 NKJV).

God's perfect wisdom, reflected in the farmer, expresses itself in as much as neither our trials nor our discipline are unending. We can be sure that if the farmer knew that black cummim was to be beaten and not threshed, so God will treat differently - will discipline differently - each type of disciple; and all "for our profit" as it yields "peaceable fruit ... even the fruit of righteousness" (Hebrews 12:10,11).

We might mention another link with Paul's letter to the Church of God in Corinth, for in chapter 3 and verse 9, the apostle describes them as 'God's tilled land'. So God's New Testament people were viewed by him in the same way as his Old Testament people were here. Let's end this chapter with another of Isaiah's inspiring glimpses into the future:

> "Behold, a king will reign in righteousness, and princes will rule with justice. A man will be as a hiding place from the wind, and a cover from the tempest, as rivers of water in a dry place, as the shadow of a great rock in a weary land... Blessed are you who sow beside all waters, who send out freely the feet of the ox and the donkey" (Isaiah 32:1,2,20 NKJV).

That's speaking of the personal, Millennial reign of Christ and his protecting care and comfort for the weary – but surely we can find in it a message of spiritual comfort for all those in the present time who are sowing the seed of God's Word.

CHAPTER 7 - ON EAGLES' WINGS

━━━

The Bible declares that God watches over his Word to perform it. In Isaiah chapters 36-39 we get an example of that. These chapters give us the historical account of the invasion of Israel by the Assyrians – just as the prophecies of the earlier chapters had been warning. At the same time this short interlude of historical data forms the basis for the rest of the message of the prophet Isaiah from chapter 40 to the end. But just as God takes pleasure in mercy rejoicing against judgement, so his message continues as one of reassurance that he would not permanently cast off his people, Israel. Chapter 40 opens with Isaiah proclaiming God's promise of future deliverance. Here was consolation: "Comfort, O comfort My people," says your God. "Speak kindly to Jerusalem" (Isaiah 40:1-2 NASB).

The word 'comfort' used here originally meant 'to cause to breathe again'. So it was real revival that was promised. One day Israel really will live again before God, agreeing with Ezekiel's picture of dry bones coming to new life. Modern preachers would do well to study the prophet's preaching here as they declare the new life that's available in Jesus Christ. Isaiah, first of all, made it quite explicit that the message was from God. He repeated the main points as a mark of his earnestness, as well as conveying a sense of urgency. What's more, God counselled him "to speak to the heart of Jerusalem." The Lord doesn't only want to offer hope, but he wants to win over our hearts while doing so.

Whenever we share with others the new life and hope that are to be found for all today in Jesus Christ, let's be sure we ask God's help to do it in a way that'll win hearts.

Isaiah's message continued:

> "A voice is calling, "Clear the way for the LORD in the wilderness; make smooth in the desert a highway for our God. Let every valley be lifted up, and every mountain and hill be made low; and let the rough ground become a plain, and the rugged terrain a broad valley; Then the glory of the LORD will be revealed, and all flesh will see [it] together; for the mouth of the LORD has spoken" (Isaiah 40:3-5 NASB).

This was like a king's courier being appointed to see that the way was put in good condition before the king travelled it. You'll remember how, in Matthew chapter 3, John the Baptist used these words ahead of the coming of Christ. John prepared the way for Jesus. The Lord encouraged the lowly, lifted them up; but he abased the proudly exalting ones; and straightened out the crooked in their dealings. In all this, God's glory was seen. But, as usual with Isaiah, there's more to come, when at Christ's second advent, the way is prepared for him to bring Israel from great tribulation into glorious millennial days. Isaiah now continues to bring God's comfort to the people, as he says:

> "Why do you say, O Jacob, and speak, O Israel: "My way is hidden from the LORD, and my just claim is passed over by my God"? Have you not known? Have

you not heard? The everlasting God, the LORD, the Creator of the ends of the earth, neither faints nor is weary. His understanding is unsearchable. He gives power to the weak, and to those who have no might He increases strength. Even the youths shall faint and be weary, and the young men shall utterly fall, but those who wait on the LORD shall renew their strength; they shall mount up with wings like eagles, they shall run and not be weary, they shall walk and not faint" (Isaiah 40:27-31 NKJV).

The situation is of a people in the grip of weariness and fainting. Their weariness produced complaints. Somehow their God had grown small. Difficulties loomed large. They had gone as far as telling God that it felt like he just didn't care. They said: "My way is hidden from the LORD, and my just claim is passed over by my God". They were doubting the scope of his knowledge; they were limiting his power to help them; and they were downplaying the extent of his concern for them.

You can probably identify with that to some extent - times when God's seemed far away, and you're left battling your problems apparently on your own. It was those kinds of feelings which produced the now quite famous little piece of poetry called 'Footprints'; you know, the one when someone dreams they're able to look back at their life's experiences charted out by following their footprints in wet sand. There are other footprints alongside theirs – which are taken to indicate the Lord's presence and help in walking with them along life's pathway.

But at times corresponding to times when there'd been difficulties in his life, the dreamer sees only one set of footprints. "Lord, why did you leave me then, just when I needed you most?" was the obvious question. The dream gives the answer, reporting it as from God: "My child, I didn't leave you at those times, it was then I was carrying you." That's just the sort of experience Israel was going through – and they, too, were asking: 'Where is God when it hurts?' God's response in Isaiah chapter 40 is to give weary Israel an invigorating vision of his majesty. They were treated to an awesome glimpse of the King of the Ages: "Have you not known? Have you not heard? The everlasting God, the LORD, the Creator of the ends of the earth, neither faints nor is weary. His understanding is unsearchable. He gives power to the weak, and to those who have no might He increases strength."

It's a glimpse that continues the marvellous vision begun earlier in Isaiah 40 where God is portrayed as the unwearied and understanding Creator – the one who has measured the waters in the hollow of his hand; and who has weighed the mountains in a balance (40:12). Then Isaiah goes on to draw his lesson from the great birds of prey: "Even the youths shall faint and be weary, and the young men shall utterly fall, but those who wait on the LORD shall renew their strength; they shall mount up with wings like eagles, they shall run and not be weary, they shall walk and not faint" (v.30,31).

Those magnificent birds expend energy – lots of it - in keeping their wings outstretched all day. They too get weary and grow faint – just like the people of Israel. But, each day at evening, the eagles come to renew their strength. All through the dark night, and on through the cold, grey gloom of the morning, these great birds simply rest patiently. They renew their strength, all the time waiting, perched on the dead branches of some skeleton tree – waiting for the sun to rise and its warmth to be felt. They know that as the sunshine floods the valleys, it'll warm the rocks and the earth, and gentle updrafts of air will start to rise above the surrounding ridges. This is the wisdom that God's given to the eagle. It knows better than to exhaust itself by beating those mighty wings in a vain effort to gain height in the cool evening air. Far better to wait for the warm morning air to rise, and then to hitch a ride on these thermal currents.

With the updraft of the thermals beneath its wings it can then soar with ease, especially having renewed its strength after a period of waiting. The eagle knew of the 'uplifting' experience of riding the thermals long before the 'hang-gliders' did. The eagle demonstrates the value of simply waiting quietly to gain strength. It restores itself. It renews its strength. It does this by waiting rather than draining itself with futile activity in a battle against the elements. Wisdom has taught it that it's better to wait. So they wait patiently without a moment's fretting or worry as to whether they're going to be able to take off and be carried aloft. They know they will – if only they wait. To wait, and not to worry: that's the secret of how the eagle renews its strength.

This is a God-given picture for you if you're weary. Or maybe for you to pass on to someone you know who's flapping about trying to make things happen in their own strength. It's a picture for everyone who's feeling the chill downdraft of doubt and discouragement – the sort of things that get us down onto the valley floor just like the eagles. The natural tendency is to do more and try harder, to work our own way through our troubles. But no, let's learn from the eagle, as the Bible directs us: this is the time to wait on the Lord. Our God is a God who works for those who wait for him – Isaiah, the prophet, again confirms this later (Isaiah 64:1-4). God intends that we soar through our difficulties, borne aloft on eagle's wings.

"Those who wait on the LORD shall renew their strength; they shall mount up with wings like eagles, they shall run and not be weary, they shall walk and not faint. So in practice, we learn to wait prayerfully on God to renew our strength." Then we rise on the wings of prayer, as the Spirit of God raises us up as overcomers – soaring through difficulties by his help.

CHAPTER 8 - SUMMONED TO APPEAR

═══

Have you ever been summoned to appear in court? Isaiah tells us how God sent out a summons to the nations of the world. "Keep silence before Me, O coastlands...let us come near together for judgment" (Isaiah 41:1 NKJV). Silence in court! It's a courtroom scene that presents itself here. As Isaiah the prophet sets the scene for us, some seven hundred years before Christ was born. It's Israel and her God on one side, and the nations and their idols on the other.

> "Present your case," says the LORD. "Bring forth your strong reasons ... bring forth and show us what will happen ... declare to us things to come. Show the things that are to come hereafter, that we may know that you are gods; yes, do good or do evil, that we may be dismayed and see it together (Isaiah 41:21-23 NKJV).

God challenges the false gods of the nations to predict future events – in fact to do anything, either good or bad – just to prove their existence by their ability to do something. It's one of the essential hallmarks of deity: to be able to forecast the future – to show the things that are to come. Of course, the idolators were ashamed at their idols' impotence, at their total inability to meet this challenge. The case, however, isn't proved until God himself can demonstrate that he can answer his own challenge.

He does that by forecasting that Cyrus, the king of Media to the north, would shortly rise to power and international influence. But God made clear here that his knowing what's going to happen isn't just because he's like some kind of spectator who has a better view than everyone else. As far as Cyrus is concerned, God makes it quite plain that God himself is writing the script for future history. History really is his story.

"I have raised up one from the north, and he shall come; from the rising of the sun he shall call on My name; and he shall come against princes as ... the potter treads clay" (Isaiah 41:25 NKJV). So it was predicted that Cyrus would overpower other kingdoms, for God was using him to fulfil his purposes. History confirms that's what happened. But as if that wasn't impressive enough, God was looking further ahead still. Cyrus, king of Media and Persia, would be his servant to do God's pleasure among the nations; but someone much greater than Cyrus was coming:

> "Behold! My Servant whom I uphold, my Elect One in whom My soul delights! I have put My Spirit upon Him; he will bring forth justice to the Gentiles. He will not cry out, nor raise His voice, nor cause His voice to be heard in the street. A bruised reed He will not break, and smoking flax He will not quench; he will bring forth justice for truth. He will not fail nor be discouraged, till He has established justice in the earth; and the coastlands shall wait for His law" (Isaiah 42:1-4 NKJV).

God was looking still further ahead, and, of course, the person in question is Jesus Christ. God demonstrates his ability to declare the future by foretelling the character of Jesus' life on earth seven hundred years in advance. It's been reckoned that some three hundred Old Testament prophecies were all fulfilled in the life, death and resurrection of Jesus Christ. That demonstrates beyond all uncertainty not only that there's a God but also that the Bible is God's Word – and it went on to say:

> "O Israel: "Fear not, for I have redeemed you; I have called you by your name; you are Mine. When you pass through the waters, I will be with you; and through the rivers, they shall not overflow you. When you walk through the fire, you shall not be burned, nor shall the flame scorch you. For I am the LORD your God, the Holy One of Israel, your Savior; I gave Egypt for your ransom, Ethiopia and Seba in your place. Since you were precious in My sight, you have been honored, and I have loved you; therefore I will give men for you, and people for your life. Everyone who is called by My name, whom I have created for My glory; I have formed him, yes, I have made him" (Isaiah 43:1-7 NKJV).

What God says here through his prophet, Isaiah, is really wonderful. When at the decree of Cyrus (Ezra 1), God brought the Jewish people back from their captivity in Babylon in the sixth century BC, God then rewarded Cyrus by permitting him and his son (Cambyses) to possess Egypt and the neighbouring kingdoms (Seba being between the White & Blue Nile, next to Ethiopia).

The possession of these lands was not simply a gift, God saw it as the ransom price paid in return for Israel's liberation. It's a marvellous demonstration of God's grace that he says of Israel that they were precious in his sight. Could any nation have failed more disastrously? Could any have grieved God more? But he says: "I have loved you". If you can identify with this inasmuch as you realize you're a sinner saved by God's grace, then I ask you to enjoy the sheer wonder that he has made a wretch – like you, like me – made a wretch his treasure. And the ransom price God paid for us was the life of his Son, Jesus. God said about Israel: "I have created him ... I have formed him ... I have made him."

With Israel, and with us, there's likely a progression of thought there. God first brings us into existence or creates us anew in Christ through faith, then transforms us by his grace, and finally, in a day to come, we'll be 'fully made', in other words, brought to perfection in every sense. But, as we usually find with Isaiah, there's a double sense to his words. God redeemed Israel historically by Cyrus, but ahead of the future millennium, he'll redeem them by Christ his Son. But more on that in a moment. For Isaiah returns next to the courtroom scene we were thinking about earlier – with God continuing to issue his challenge:

> "Let all the nations be gathered together, and let the people be assembled. Who among them can declare this, and show us former things? Let them bring out their witnesses ... "You are My witnesses," says the

LORD, "And My servant whom I have chosen, that you may know and believe Me, and understand that I am He. Before Me there was no God formed, nor shall there be after Me. I, even I, am the LORD, and besides Me there is no savior ... you are My witnesses," says the LORD, "that I am God" (Isaiah 43:9-12 NKJV).

In the context of Isaiah, the witnesses to the Lord, to Jehovah, are none other than the actual nation of Israel. In demonstrating his existence and sovereignty over all of history, God calls on Israel as his star witness. The story of the nation of Israel is a monumental witness to God. The events of the second half of the last century definitely recall to mind Isaiah's prophecy: "I will bring your descendants from the east, and gather you from the west; I will say to the north, 'Give them up!' And to the south, 'Do not keep them back!' Bring My sons from afar, and My daughters from the ends of the earth'" (Isaiah 43:5,6). And the story's not finished yet as God promises:

"I will do a new thing, now it shall spring forth; shall you not know it? I will even make a road in the wilderness and rivers in the desert. The beast of the field will honor Me, the jackals and the ostriches, because I give waters in the wilderness and rivers in the desert, to give drink to My people, My chosen. This people I have formed for Myself; they shall declare My praise."

Throughout Isaiah, there's mention of this new world order that's coming. Israel will declare God's praise in the centre of the earth, a world that's transformed with wild animals becoming peaceful and deserts becoming fertile. None of this is what Israel deserves, for God himself brings the following charges against her:

> "But you have not called upon Me ... O Israel. You have not ... honored Me with your sacrifices. I have not caused you to serve with grain offerings, nor wearied you with incense ... but you have burdened Me with your sins, you have wearied Me with your iniquities. "I, even I, am He who blots out your transgressions for My own sake; and I will not remember your sins" (Isaiah 43:18-25 NKJV).

Even though they've not honoured him, God will not deal with them as their sins deserve – just as he won't deal with us as our sins deserve if we turn to him and appeal to his mercy in Jesus Christ. 'You have burdened Me with your sins', God says to Israel, and our minds can't help turning to the cross where, according to the Bible, Jesus bore our sins in his body on the tree. When we turn and trust in him, God promises to forgive and forget our sins too. It's time to judge the case for Christ and Christianity and reach your verdict!

CHAPTER 9 - PATTERN SERVANT

====

Through the prophet Isaiah, God addresses Israel as his servant. He speaks about "My servant, Israel". But at times it becomes clear that it's really the Lord Jesus that's in view as God's servant – as when, for example, the servant in question is given the task of gathering and restoring Israel. That kind of ambiguity shouldn't disturb us, for even Israel, when she's restored to God, can only act as God's servant in the earth inasmuch as she's identified finally with Jesus Christ as her true Messiah.

That's a good reminder to us that any service we do for God, can only be in the strength of our association with the Lord. But, with that reminder, let's come to the forty-ninth chapter of Isaiah where we find the Lord Jesus - sometimes identified with Israel - and being described as God's servant: "Listen to me, O islands, and pay attention, you peoples from afar. The LORD called me from the womb; from the body of My mother He named me." This is a message that's directed outwards into all the world. God has only one saviour for the whole world – someone who was named by God himself straight from the body of his mother. The birth of Jesus Christ fulfilled that as we read in Matthew's Gospel:

"Now the birth of Jesus Christ was as follows. When His mother Mary had been betrothed to Joseph, before they came together she was found to be with child by the Holy Spirit. And Joseph her husband, being a righteous man, and not wanting to disgrace her, desired to put her away secretly. But when he had considered this, behold, an angel of the Lord appeared to him in a dream, saying, "Joseph, son of David, do not be afraid to take Mary as your wife; for that which has been conceived in her is of the Holy Spirit. And she will bear a Son; and you shall call His name Jesus, for it is He who will save His people from their sins" (Matthew 1:18-21 NASB).

"Well might Mary's relative, Elizabeth, say to her: "Blessed among women are you, and blessed is the fruit of your womb!" (Luke 1:42 NASB). In this miraculous way, Isaiah's words came to pass that God's great servant would be called from the womb, and named from his mother's body as the beginning of the New Testament record shows Jesus was. Right at the other end of the New Testament, the apostle John describes the risen and glorified Lord Jesus who appeared to him in a vision as having a mouth associated with a two-edged sword (Revelation 1:16). Later, in that last book of the Bible, he writes:

"And I saw heaven opened; and behold, a white horse, and He who sat upon it is called Faithful and True; and in righteousness He judges and wages war ... And the armies which are in heaven, clothed in fine linen, white and clean, were following Him on white horses.

And from His mouth comes a sharp sword, so that
with it He may smite the nations" (Revelation
19:11-15 NASB).

The world's still waiting for this second intervention by Jesus
Christ – when he's coming back to judge the earth – but the
picture of the sword proceeding from his mouth gives us another
connection with Isaiah's description of the Lord Jesus, when
Isaiah says: "And He has made My mouth like a sharp sword; in
the shadow of His hand He has concealed me."

Isaiah saw the time ahead too, the same as John, and he
prophesied of how the Lord will strike the earth with the rod of
his mouth (Isaiah 11:4), and cause his voice of authority to be
heard (Isaiah 30:30). This will take place when the Lord comes
to rescue Israel out of deep trouble at the time of the end. In that
day, the Lord's identity will be hidden from no-one. How unlike
his first advent! Especially when we think of the greater part of
his life which was lived outside the public domain. That reminds
me of how Isaiah goes on to say: "He has also made me a select
(or polished) arrow; He has hidden me in His quiver."

The Gospels have practically nothing to say of the Lord's early
life. These were hidden years of preparation in which the Lord
was made ready to be sent out for the great purpose God had in
his life. The picture here is of an arrow, made ready through the
work of polishing, and kept ready for use, ready to hit the mark
when the time came.

It was like that with Jesus Christ. There was no resistance, no roughness, nothing to deflect him from the bull's eye. His hidden years of preparation were years hidden with God, kept in "God's quiver", always closely in communion with his Father – as we see from God's words to his servant: "You are My servant, Israel, in whom I will show My glory." But I said, "I have toiled in vain, I have spent My strength for nothing and vanity; yet surely the justice due to me is with the LORD, and My reward with My God."

Here's an example of Christ identifying with his people. And Israel, the Jewish people, will only ever display God's glory through their identification with Christ – and it'll be especially true in the future. Before Israel's future glory there'll be some very bitter experiences for them – which is why the verse strikes a note that's almost one of despondency: "I have toiled in vain ... spent my strength for nothing". The pressure on Israel that we see today is going to increase. The Bible predicts her land will again be invaded, and once again subjected to occupying forces. In those dark days, the efforts even of a loyal core in the Israelite nation will seem to have been in vain, and for nothing. But then, elsewhere, the Bible predicts their deliverance at the hand of Jesus Christ.

Their trial will have prepared them so that the Lord can finally be glorified in them in the centre of this earth during the coming thousand-year reign of Christ. Is there not yet another hint of what we're calling "double vision" here? Was there any sense, I wonder, in which the same sentiment of seemingly working for no return could have been applied to the Lord Jesus? It appeared that way to others during the time of his rejection by Israel at his first advent.

The Lord himself, of course, was never discouraged, but recognized in faith throughout his sufferings that the justice and reward due to him were with God. And we thank God his work was not in vain – far from it! Let's encourage ourselves as we reflect on Israel's experience – and more especially on our Lord's - that even when things seem most bleak or discouraging or even downright wrong, we can still, in faith, leave the outcome with God - that in us, ultimately, he'll be glorified. But the servant Isaiah's describing has still got more to say: "Now says the LORD, who formed me from the womb to be His servant, to bring Jacob back to Him, in order that Israel might be gathered to Him (for I am honored in the sight of the LORD, and My God is My strength)"

As far as Israel's concerned, this work of the Lord Jesus as God's servant might not yet seem to have been effective, but it is he, and he alone, who will bring the nation of Israel back to God. And it's this work that specially pleases the Father (see the word 'for'), and in response the Lord here declares his own delight as reflecting the Father's pleasure in him. For he says: "I am honoured in the sight of the LORD" – and God says, "It is too small a thing that you should be My servant to ... restore the preserved ones of Israel; I will also make you a light of the nations so that My salvation may reach to the end of the earth."

This prophecy will be fulfilled both now in the spread of the Gospel, and then again when Christ rules on earth after his second advent. Jesus Christ will restore Israel to himself and in him all the nations of the earth will be blessed as was promised to Abraham long ago. Thus says the LORD: "In a favorable time I have answered You, and in a day of salvation I have helped you." (Isaiah 49:1-8 NASB)

It was in an acceptable time that God raised his servant Jesus from the dead, and so delivered him from all the trials of his life on earth. But just as Isaiah identifies Israel here with Christ the servant, so Israel, too, will one day be delivered when God himself judges the time to be acceptable to him. That's in the future time of the end, but, now, on an individual basis, the New Testament (2 Corinthians 6:2) applies this great verse from Isaiah to all of us today when it says: "At an acceptable time I listened to you, and on the day of salvation I helped you" - telling us that now is the acceptable time for any of us personally to receive the salvation that's on offer in Jesus Christ.

CHAPTER 10 - THE CROSS

━━━

The feet of those who carry the good news of Jesus Christ are lovely in the sight of the Lord who died to provide both the message and the messengers. That's the encouraging thought we lead off with today, from Isaiah 52:7: "How lovely on the mountains are the feet of him who brings good news, who announces peace and brings good news of happiness, who announces salvation, {and} says to Zion, "Your God reigns!"

The message announces three blessings: peace, happiness and salvation. Isaiah is projecting us away into the future. This is not the outcome of any human road map to peace for the city of Jerusalem. After many false dawns, when people cried out "peace and safety" (1 Thessalonians 5:3), finally the "sun of righteousness" (Malachi 4:2) will rise upon Jerusalem's inhabitants, and the Lord's coming at that time will be as "a dawn prepared" (Hosea 6:3, LXX). At long last, the city of Jerusalem – and with her, all the world - will understand that humanity can never be its own saviour. The promise of "peace and safety" is a lie, unless it's God's own work to bring it about. But Isaiah sees that one day God will rule in Jerusalem:

> "...when the LORD restores Zion ... shout joyfully together, you waste places of Jerusalem; for the LORD has comforted His people, He has redeemed

> Jerusalem. The LORD has bared His holy arm in the sight of all the nations, that all the ends of the earth may see the salvation of our God ..." (v.8-10).

Who is it who'll at last end the state of crisis in the Middle East? Isaiah reveals the divine identity of the deliverer, for it's said to be the LORD who restores Zion. Deliverance from Babylon in the sixth century was the starting point for this prophecy, but really Isaiah doesn't mention that event again, his focus is more and more on a deliverance that's still future and one which will be final. Now Isaiah further identifies exactly who the deliverer is. For God is reported as saying that the deliverer, his: "... servant will prosper, He will be high and lifted up, and greatly exalted. Just as many were astonished at you, My people, so His appearance was marred more than any man, and His form more than the sons of men. Thus He will startle many nations, kings will shut their mouths on account of Him" (v.13-15).

In other words, the deliverer is the same one who became more marred than the men whom he befriended. It's none other than Jesus Christ. Many were astonished at his disfigurement at his first advent - and Isaiah tells us - many others will be just as startled - rendered speechless in fact - by his glorious appearance at his second advent, when he returns to this earth at the head of the armies of heaven to liberate Jerusalem. With these few words, Isaiah describes the humiliation of the Lord Jesus when he was crucified in weakness, followed by his glory when he comes back in the future to display his power. But, in his fifty-third chapter, Isaiah expands on Jesus Christ's humiliation and exaltation in much more detail:

> "He was despised and forsaken of men, a man of sorrows, and acquainted with grief; and like one from whom men hide their face, He was despised, and we did not esteem Him" (v.3).

The strength of this language is striking for the depth of feeling it expresses. Remember the raw emotions when Joseph's brothers were brought face to face with Egypt's second-in-command – and then suddenly confronted with the revelation that this seemingly all-powerful person was their own brother whom they'd treated so despicably in the past?

Well, those feelings must surely pale into nothingness compared with what Isaiah's describing here. In his prophetic vision, Isaiah is looking ahead to a future time when a deliverer comes to liberate Jerusalem. Even repentant Israel could never be fully prepared for this meeting with their deliverer – the one they had earlier crucified at his first advent. They'd regarded him as nothing, as one who was unbearable to look at. Listen to the depth of their remorse in that coming day: "... we ourselves esteemed Him stricken, smitten of God, and afflicted. But He was pierced through for our transgressions, He was crushed for our iniquities" (vv.4,5).

The sufferings of Christ's cross are now in view. Israel will confess they were of a totally different nature from what they'd supposed them to have been two thousand years ago. The majority of the nation, two thousand years ago, had followed their religious leaders and considered Jesus Christ to be a blasphemer when he claimed to be equal with God.

That's why he was suffering, cursed on the cross, they thought – the sufferings they witnessed him going through were, they thought, the due reward of his blasphemy. But, by the time of Armageddon, they know differently. "We...esteemed him...smitten of God' (for blasphemy), they said, 'But he was pierced through (on the cross) for our transgressions', our sins, our wrongs. What a complete about-face in their thoughts – it's one that illustrates repentance: the kind of turn around we need in our own thinking so as to confront what the cross means to us in terms of our relationship with God. If you've previously thought little or nothing of Jesus Christ, then I urge you to repent, and see him crucified to take the blame for all the bad things you've ever thought and said and done.

"... the chastening for our well-being fell upon Him, and by His scourging [or with his stripes] we are healed." The literal translation of Isaiah's words here would be singular – a single bruise or stroke was inflicted upon Jesus Christ at the cross. So this wouldn't seem to be referring to the Roman scourging he received. True, that was fearful enough, for the flesh was usually cut away from the breast as well as the back, exposing the bones – which the book of Psalms indicates actually happened in the case of Christ (Psalm 22:17). But this singular expression – the wound – or the stripe – that brings spiritual healing to all who believe – seems to be a clear reference to the stroke of divine judgement. 'That fearful stroke' – the hymnwriter says – 'That fearful stroke, it fell on Him, and life for us was won.' By contrast the word describing Jesus' death is, in fact, a plural word: "His grave was assigned with wicked men, yet He was with a rich man in His death, because He had done no violence, nor was there any deceit in His mouth" (v.9).

The suggestion is that the use of the plural word for death implies the violent as well as the comprehensive nature of his death. The death he died, he died for all. And it was a death that all the different kinds of Old Testament animal sacrifices had prefigured. His one death answered to them all in what it accomplished for God and for us, as:

> "the LORD was pleased to crush Him, putting Him to grief; [when His soul shall make an offering for sin], He will see His offspring, He will prolong His days, and the good pleasure of the LORD will prosper in His hand. As a result of the anguish of His soul, He will see it and be satisfied; by His knowledge the Righteous One, My servant, will justify the many, as He will bear their iniquities. Therefore, I will allot Him a portion with the great, and He will divide the booty with the strong; because He poured out [his soul] to death, and was numbered with the transgressors; yet He himself bore the sin of many, and interceded for the transgressors" (Isaiah 53:10-12 NASB).

In those words from Isaiah there are three references to the soul of Christ. Someone has said that the soul of his suffering was the suffering of his soul. By that they meant that the heart of Christ's sufferings wasn't what he suffered in terms of the scourging and the nails or even the excruciating, suffocating act of crucifixion itself, but we're back to that 'fearful stroke' from above, that descended in the darkness of his cross, and which no human eye saw. It was then he substituted for sinners in bearing before a holy God the legal consequences of our sins. Sin's penalty is separation from God (Romans 6:23) and that was the horror of his cross experience – it was being forsaken by God. Because the soul of Christ experienced the forsaking of God at the cross, all who turn to God, believing what truly did take place at the cross, will never themselves have to experience what it means to be forsaken by God.

Instead, Calvary's dark night of suffering which the Saviour endured guarantees to all who believe that they, like Jerusalem, will experience "a dawn prepared" – one that extends to a bright eternal day in the sunshine of God's presence. I trust you've turned about in your thoughts and fully realized that Jesus Christ was wounded for your transgressions ...

CHAPTER 11 - THE RUNNER

In the last chapter, when dealing with chapter 53 of Isaiah's prophecy, we were brought face to face with the cross of Jesus Christ – as predicted hundreds of years beforehand; and as finally understood by Israel nationally some time in the future. Everyone, whether Jew or Gentile, who's come to know what the cross means for them personally, has known what it means to shout for joy. And so, in the very next chapter of Isaiah's prophecy, that's exactly what Israel is told to do!

> "'Shout for joy, O barren one, you who have borne no child; break forth into joyful shouting and cry aloud, you who have not travailed; for the sons of the desolate one will be more numerous than the sons of the married woman,' says the LORD" (Isaiah 54:1 NASB).

In the context of Israel, this might make us think of the situation of their great founding father – the situation of Abraham, or more specifically: that of Abraham's wife, Sarah. Sarah couldn't have children. Her barrenness must've been a real trial for her. When, with God's long-promised intervention, she did at last give birth in old age: what exclamations of joy there were! Like Sarah, Israel will one day come to the end of a great trial, and will finally rejoice in joyful appreciation of all the cross of Jesus Christ means for her. She'll shout for joy in that day! But, before that her trial will become very intense indeed. Even now Israel is storm-tossed and afflicted, as Isaiah long ago predicted – and things are going to get still worse:

> "O afflicted one, storm-tossed, and not comforted, behold, I will set your stones in antimony, and your foundations I will lay in sapphires. Moreover, I will make your battlements of rubies, and your gates of crystal, and your entire wall of precious stones" (Isaiah 54:11-17).

Things will get even stormier before they get better. In context, it's speaking about Jerusalem battered and afflicted by the Great Tribulation: "O afflicted one, storm-tossed, and not comforted" (NASB). But when that storm is over, she comes through in Millennial days to reflect God's glory like a glittering jewel: "Behold, I will lay your stones with colorful gems, and lay your foundations with sapphires" (Isaiah 54:11 NKJV).

That will be the time when Christ reigns on this earth for a thousand years. But at the moment, the storm-clouds are gathering for Israel on the road to Armageddon. Still, God assures her "No weapon that is formed against you shall prosper". And so after a time of great trial, an Israelite core that proves loyal to God will be resplendent in glory when Christ reigns on earth. But surely this verse also has an application to the storm-tossed Christian who's now passing through trials of various kinds. If you're passing through a time of difficulty, and the end is not yet in sight, try to remember that God's ultimate purpose is that we'll show forth His glory – sparkling all the more with the glory of God like gemstones in the sunshine as a result of present trials! Hard to appreciate when we're care-worn, I know, but this is the promise of God's Word (1 Peter 1:7). Through Isaiah, God goes on to give reassurance that what he says will come to pass, it'll take place. He says:

> "For as the rain and the snow come down from heaven, and do not return there without watering the earth, and making it bear and sprout, and furnishing seed to the sower and bread to the eater; So shall My word be which goes forth from My mouth; it shall not return to me empty, without accomplishing what I desire, and without succeeding {in the matter} for which I sent it" (Isaiah 55:10-11 NASB).

To make the point dramatically clear, God personifies his word as a messenger which he sends out. The picture is of God's Word itself going out as a swift runner. In the New Testament, God speaks the same way through the apostle Paul when he writes: "Finally, brethren, pray for us, that the word of the Lord may run swiftly and be glorified." (2 Thessalonians 3:1 NKJV). Once again, the Word of the Lord is personified as a runner. Paul's request that he makes of his friends in the Church of God in Thessalonica was that they should pray that the Word of the Lord – in other words the message he preached – might "run and be glorified." What exactly is Paul's picture here?

He often made reference to the Greek Games, and I think he's now again picturing the Word being like the athlete running in with the Olympian torch to a glorious reception. In fact, that was how the Word had been received at Thessalonica. The people there had been wonderfully saved through faith in the Word of Christ.

Thinking of God's Word going out like a runner, made me think of a famous runner of modern times: Carl Lewis. At twenty years of age he was the world's number one in the 100 metres (as well as the long jump). Ten years later, in 1991, he exploded out of the starting blocks and broke the world record for the 100 metres in a time of 9.86 seconds. It's been said of him that no athlete in history has performed better for longer. In the 1984 Olympics at Los Angeles he won four gold medals; he struck gold twice more in the Seoul Olympics of '88; then added another two gold medals to his tally in Barcelona in 1992; and finally a single gold medal (for the long jump) at the 1996 Atlanta Olympics.

That's a total of nine Olympic gold medals, but he can only display eight of them today. When his father died in 1987, and Carl Lewis with his family was filing past the open coffin, he put his then one and only 100 metres gold medal (his other gold medals were for different events) into his dead father's hand in the coffin. His mother heard him say quietly: 'I want you to have this 'cos it was your favourite event'. His mom looked at him as if to say, 'You can't do that!'; but Lewis just said: 'Don't worry, Mom. I'll get another' – and he did! That's Carl Lewis the runner. But Isaiah the Old Testament prophet, joined by the apostle Paul in the New Testament, have both been describing the Word of God, the Lord's message, as a runner. It runs so as to put a 'golden deposit' into the hands of dead sinners.

Let me explain what I mean by that. We're dead in our sins, the Bible explains (Ephesians 2:1), before such time as the truth of the Good News of God's Grace comes to us. God's Good News isn't only a message about receiving God's forgiveness and new life in Jesus, but it also instructs us how we're to live that life (Titus 2:12) by serving the living and true God (1 Thessalonians 1:9).

This instruction on how we're to serve God as disciples of Christ is given through the writing down of the apostles' teaching in the New Testament of the Bible we have in our hand. In that Bible we're introduced to a young man, Timothy, who was privileged to have the apostle Paul as his mentor. Paul spoke to him of the need for him to get a grasp of this teaching, the faith of the Gospel, as he called it. Paul described it as a 'treasure', a beautiful 'deposit' which is entrusted to us to really hold onto. So if God's Word has come to us, and we've received it by his grace, then that's something absolutely glorious. It's something pictured in the Bible as being like the Olympic runner coming into the stadium.

Maybe the athlete is holding the Olympic torch, or maybe completing the marathon, and entering the stadium for the last lap. The crowd's up on its feet clapping – it's a glorious reception. God has reserved for himself human lives today where God's Word enters and is glorified as they receive it. From being 'dead in sins', all those who receive the Word as the Lord's message, receive life – and have a life to give in the service of God, following Christ. All the instruction they need from God's Word is placed within their reach - surely we can say that's a 'golden deposit' in the hand of a once dead sinner! Only this week, I've been sent a bundle of products. They're software packages for my computer. There's only one that I think could be useful to me, but I'm being sent about eight different packages on approval. Even if, at the end of the day, I choose to buy none of them, three of the packages will be mine to keep anyway, absolutely free.

We've been thinking about the teaching or the faith of the gospel which instructs us how to live to serve God as disciples of Jesus Christ. But even if we don't hold onto the deposit of teaching, even if we don't keep the faith, we still retain our salvation as a free gift from God. But, just as the computer software people obviously intend me to buy all the titles they send, God wants – he intends - us to value and treasure the whole 'golden' deposit that's been put into our hands – or at least it's been placed there if God's Word has been clearly and faithfully preached to us. Isaiah's vision, his words which we started with, were directed towards Israel primarily, but we've seen there can be an application for us too – in our joyful response to the cross of Christ; in anticipating the glory after stormy trials; and in giving God's Word a glorious reception in our hearts.

CHAPTER 12 - WONDERFUL TIMES AHEAD

===

In this book we've talked a lot about Israel, because the main thrust of Isaiah's prophecy focused on Jerusalem and Israel, the land and its people. By the word of the Lord, Isaiah knew terrible times were coming upon Jerusalem. But he was further back in time than prophet Jeremiah, and it's as if this longer-range perspective enabled Isaiah to see ahead to the recovery and better times that lay beyond. As we draw our look at the book of Isaiah to a close, one thing stands out clearly: the longer-term future for Jerusalem is glorious - for God has promised his help: "... until her righteousness goes forth like brightness, and her salvation like a torch that is burning. And the nations ... see your righteousness, and all kings your glory" (Isaiah 62:1).

Instead of Israel needing mediators in that coming day, God says to them "you will be called the priests of the LORD" (Isaiah 61:6), "decked" (Isaiah 61:10) as a priest (as well as a bridegroom, from the meaning of the word), she will be a "royal diadem" – or priestly mitre – "in the hand of [her] God" (Isaiah 62:3). All the nations of the earth will come to her to learn the ways of God (see Isaiah 2). More than ever before, Israel will fulfil the words God spoke to them at the time the ten commandments were given: "Now therefore, if you will indeed obey My voice and keep My covenant, then you shall be a special treasure to Me above all people; for all the earth is Mine. And you shall be to Me a kingdom of priests and a holy nation" (Exodus 19:5-6 NKJV). But there's something even more amazing here. Isaiah even speaks of the actions of non-Jews using the language of priestly service. In his final chapter, he writes:

> "the time is coming to gather all nations and tongues. And they shall come and see My [the Lord's] glory. "Then they [the Gentile peoples] shall bring all your brethren [the Jews] from all the nations as a grain offering to the LORD ... just as the sons of Israel bring their grain offering in a clean vessel to the house of the LORD" (Isaiah 66:18-20 NASB).

I couldn't help thinking of the words of Paul, when in the fifteenth chapter of his letter to the Romans, he spoke of the: "... grace that was given [him] from God, to be a minister of Christ Jesus to the Gentiles, ministering as a priest the gospel of God, that [my] offering of the Gentiles might become acceptable, sanctified by the Holy Spirit" (Romans 15:15-16 NASB).

Here was a Jew bringing his offering of Gentiles to God; but when Christ reigns and gathers the nations to see his glory, the Gentile peoples will come bringing their offering of Jews to God! Other words of the apostle Paul in Romans relate to this time in the future. In chapter 11, Paul said of the Jewish people: "... because of their transgression [in rejecting Christ], salvation has come to the Gentiles to make Israel envious. But if their [Israel's] transgression means riches for the world, and their loss means riches for the Gentiles, how much greater riches will their fulness bring!" (Romans 11:11-12 NIV).

The fullness of Israel will bring an even greater measure of blessing to Gentiles on this earth in the future. Isaiah gives a description of what life will be like on this earth in the future when Jesus Christ is reigning. He writes:

"They shall not build, and another inhabit, they shall not plant, and another eat; for as the lifetime of a tree, [so shall be] the days of My people, and My chosen ones shall wear out the work of their hands. They shall not labor in vain, or bear [children] for calamity; for they are the offspring of those blessed by the LORD, and their descendants with them ...The wolf and the lamb shall graze together, and the lion shall eat straw like the ox; and dust shall be the serpent's food. They shall do no evil or harm in all My holy mountain," says the LORD (Isaiah 65:22-25 NASB).

Some might question whether that's realistic, preferring to understand it as poetic licence perhaps, but earlier this century, a female African lion, born and raised in America, lived her entire lifetime of nine years without ever eating meat. Alarmed by scientific reports that carnivorous animals could not live without meat, her owners went to great lengths to try to coax 'Little Tyke', as their lion was called, to eat meat – but all to no avail. Even when a single drop of blood was placed in her drinking milk, she refused to touch it. Yet one of America's 'most able zoo curators' apparently said that the lioness 'was the best of her species he'd ever viewed.' Large numbers of visitors to the ranch where 'Little Tyke' was kept were drawn by the prospect of seeing 'the lion that lives with the lamb' – a similar situation to the prophecies of Isaiah (Isaiah 11:6).

This lioness lived placidly among sheep and cattle. To condition her stomach the lioness would spend an hour at a time eating the succulent tall grass in the fields – which vividly recalls Isaiah chapter 65, verse 25: "the lion will eat straw like the ox." Wonderful times lie ahead for this earth, with justice and peace the order of the day, and all of nature in harmony: it'll be like paradise regained. But no humanist agenda will bring about this 'golden age' – only the personal return of Jesus Christ. The victory that transforms Jerusalem from being like a ship on a storm-tossed sea to being like sparkling gems on Aaron's priestly breastplate is not her own. Isaiah brings us something like an interview with Israel's rescuer. For chapter 63 has opened with question and answer: "Who is this who comes from Edom, with garments of glowing colors from Bozrah, this One who is majestic in His apparel, marching in the greatness of His strength? It is I who speak in righteousness, mighty to save."

In other words, the answer is: it's the Lord Jesus Christ. He is asked: "Why is your apparel red, and your garments like the one who treads in the wine press?" Back comes the answer: "I have trodden the wine trough alone, and from the peoples there was no man with me. I also trod them in My anger, and trampled them in My wrath; and their lifeblood is sprinkled on My garments, and I stained all My raiment" (Isaiah 63:1-4 NASB). There seems little doubt that Isaiah's prophecy here is looking way ahead to the end-time campaign of Armageddon as described in the Bible's very last book. Isaiah's words match those of the apostle John in Revelation: "And the wine press was trodden outside the city, and blood came out from the wine press, up to the horses' bridles, for a distance of two hundred miles" (Revelation 14:20 NASB).

Earlier in his prophecy, Isaiah has predicted once before the doom of Edom, and Bozrah in particular: "The sword of the LORD is filled with blood, it is made overflowing with fatness, with the blood of lambs and goats, with the fat of the kidneys of rams. For the LORD has a sacrifice in Bozrah, and a great slaughter in the land of Edom (Isaiah 34:5-8 NKJV). With his words, the words of Jeremiah are in agreement. For he says: "Concerning Edom ... I have sworn by myself, saith the LORD, that Bozrah shall become a desolation, a reproach, a waste, and a curse; and all the cities thereof shall be perpetual wastes" (Jeremiah 49:7-22 KJV).

This is probably at the time Daniel (Daniel 11:42-45) foresaw when the Antichrist comes to his end with none to help him. If this takes place south of Israel in the wilderness of Kadesh region (as Bible scholar W.E. Vine says), then the 200 miles the book of Revelation talks about would take us up north to Sirion in Lebanon –and so let's conclude with a celebration of the triumph of the Lord's word and voice from Psalm 29:

> "The voice of the LORD breaks the cedars; yes, the LORD breaks in pieces the cedars of Lebanon. And He makes Lebanon skip like a calf, and Sirion like a young wild ox. The voice of the LORD hews out flames of fire. The voice of the LORD shakes the wilderness; the LORD shakes the wilderness of

Kadesh ... The LORD will give strength to His people; the LORD will bless His people with peace" (NASB).

Isaiah's message, too, ends with peace – for Israel and all nations – on an earth ruled by the victorious Christ when war is ended for a thousand years.

Did you love *Double Vision: Hidden Meanings in the Prophecy of Isaiah*? Then you should read *Minor Prophets: Major Issues!* by Brian Johnston!

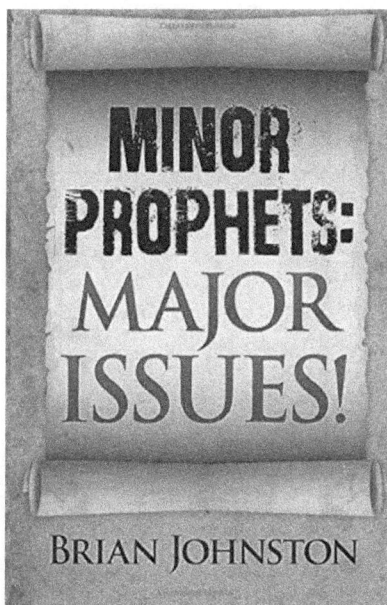

The so-called "Minor Prophets" of the Old Testament of our Bibles, such as Nahum, Micah and Malachi, are often overlooked because of their brevity and also because they might seem irrelevant to Christians of today.

Brian Johnston shows how inaccurate this perception is by pointing out in this Old Testament commentary that, although these books do not perhaps provide much in the way of a biography of each prophet – the content of what they spoke was not only vitally important to the peoples of that era, but they also raise very major issues that are absolutely relevant to believers today.

Such issues identified in this Bible survey are: injustice, suffering, unfaithfulness, abandonment, corruption, compassion, arrogance and wrong priorities.

This concise Bible overview and study guide to the Minor Prophets is designed to unlock this important part of the Bible and challenge your own experience as a disciple of Jesus Christ.

Also by Brian Johnston

Healthy Churches - God's Bible Blueprint For Growth

Hope for Humanity: God's Fix for a Broken World

First Corinthians: Nothing But Christ Crucified

Bible Answers to Listeners' Questions

Living in God's House: His Design in Action

Christianity 101: Seven Bible Basics

Nights of Old: Bible Stories of God at Work

Daniel Decoded: Deciphering Bible Prophecy

A Test of Commitment: 15 Challenges to Stimulate Your Devotion to Christ

John's Epistles - Certainty in the Face of Change

If Atheism Is True...

8 Amazing Privileges of God's People: A Bible Study of Romans 9:4-5

Learning from Bible Grandparents

Increasing Your Christian Footprint

Christ-centred Faith

Mindfulness That Jesus Endorses

Amazing Grace! Paul's Gospel Message to the Galatians

Abraham: Friend of God

The Future in Bible Prophecy

Unlocking Hebrews

Learning How To Pray - From the Lord's Prayer

About the Bush: The Five Excuses of Moses
The Five Loves of God
Deepening Our Relationship With Christ
Really Good News For Today!
A Legacy of Kings - Israel's Chequered History
Minor Prophets: Major Issues!
The Tabernacle - God's House of Shadows
Tribes and Tribulations - Israel's Predicted Personalities
Once Saved, Always Saved - The Reality of Eternal Security
After God's Own Heart : The Life of David
Jesus: What Does the Bible Really Say?
God: His Glory, His Building, His Son
The Feasts of Jehovah in One Hour
Knowing God - Reflections on Psalm 23
Praying with Paul
Get Real ... Living Every Day as an Authentic Follower of
Christ
A Crisis of Identity
Double Vision: Hidden Meanings in the Prophecy of Isaiah
Samson: A Type of Christ
Great Spiritual Movements
Take Your Mark's Gospel
Total Conviction - 4 Things God Wants You To Be Fully
Convinced About
Esther: A Date With Destiny
Experiencing God in Ephesians
James - Epistle of Straw?
The Supremacy of Christ
The Visions of Zechariah
Encounters at the Cross
Five Sacred Solos - The Truths That the Reformation Recovered

Kingdom of God: Past, Present or Future?
Overcoming Objections to Christian Faith
Stronger Than the Storm - The Last Words of Jesus
Fencepost Turtles - People Placed by God
Five Woman and a Baby - The Genealogy of Jesus
Pure Milk - Nurturing New Life in Jesus
Jesus: Son Over God's House
Salt and the Sacrifice of Christ
The Glory of God
The Way: Being a New Testament Disciple
Power Outage - Christianity Unplugged
Windows to Faith: Insights for the Inquisitive
Home Truths
60 Minutes to Raise the Dead

About the Author

Born and educated in Scotland, Brian worked as a government scientist until God called him into full-time Christian ministry on behalf of the Churches of God (www.churchesofgod.info). His voice has been heard on Search For Truth radio broadcasts for over 30 years (visit www.searchfortruth.podbean.com) during which time he has been an itinerant Bible teacher throughout the UK and Canada. His evangelical and missionary work outside the UK is primarily in Belgium and The Philippines. He is married to Rosemary, with a son and daughter.

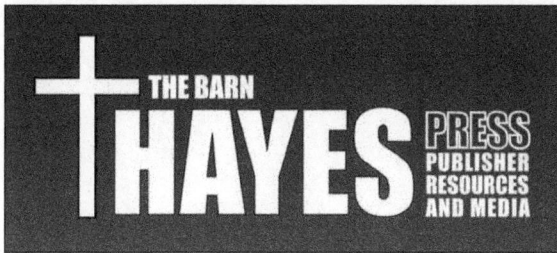

About the Publisher

Hayes Press (www.hayespress.org) is a registered charity in the United Kingdom, whose primary mission is to disseminate the Word of God, mainly through literature. It is one of the largest distributors of gospel tracts and leaflets in the United Kingdom, with over 100 titles and hundreds of thousands despatched annually. In addition to paperbacks and eBooks, Hayes Press also publishes Plus Eagles Wings, a fun and educational Bible magazine for children, and Golden Bells, a popular daily Bible reading calendar in wall or desk formats. Also available are over 100 Bibles in many different versions, shapes and sizes, Bible text posters and much more!